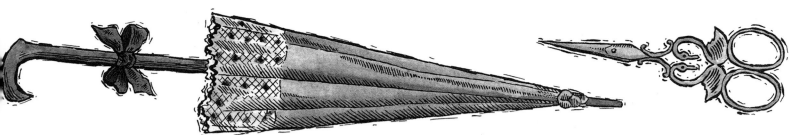

THE FACTS ABOUT

THE VICTORIANS

Kay Woodward

HODDER
Wayland

an imprint of Hodder Children's Books

First published in 2001 by Hodder Wayland as
What Do We Know About the Victorians? by
Richard Tames

This differentiated text version by Kay
Woodward, published in 2005 by Hodder
Wayland, an imprint of Hodder Children's Books

Hodder Children's Books
A division of Hodder Headline
Limited
338 Euston Road
London NW1 3BH

Designer and illustrator: Celia Hart
Layout for this edition: Jane Hawkins
Editor for this edition: Hayley Leach
Cover design: Hodder Wayland

British Library Cataloguing in Publication Data
Woodward, Kay
> The facts about the Victorians
> 1.Great Britain – Civilization – 19th century – Juvenile literature
> 2.Great Britain – History – Victoria, 1837-1901 – Juvenile literature
> I.Title
> 941'.081

ISBN 075024763 0

Printed in China by WKT Company Ltd

The author and publisher would like to thank the following for allowing their pictures to be
reproduced in this publication: p16 (Harrogate Museums and Art Gallery), 17(t) (Royal Holloway
and Bedford New College, Surrey), 20(b) and 25(b) (Christopher Wood Gallery, London), 43(tr)
(private collection); The Thomas Cook Travel Archive, p41(b); The Co-operative Union Ltd, p15(c);
courtesy of the Dickens' House Museum, London, p36(r); E.T. Archive, p22(l), 23(b), 26(r) (Sir
Benjamin Stone Collection), 39(b); Mary Evans Picture Library, cover, p14(b), 20(t), 27(b), 36(l),
41(t); Fine Art Photographs, p9(t), 12(b) courtesy of Fine Art of Oakham, 21(t), 25(t) (N.R.Omell
Gallery, London); Fitzwilliam Museum, University of Cambridge, p40(l); Guy's Hospital, London,
Evelina Children's Hospital Appeal, p31(b); Hulton Deutsch Collection, p9(bl), 9(br), 17(b), 26(l),
33(t), 39(t); Leeds City Art Galleries, p34; Manchester City Art Galleries, p 23(t) The Dinner Hour,
Wigan by Eyre Crowe; The Mansell Collection, p15(b), 19(t), 21(b), 33(b), 37(r), 38(r); William Morris
Gallery, endpapers; Museum of London, p14(t); courtesy of the Director, National Army Museum London,
p42; National Maritime Museum, London, p43(b), National Portrait Gallery, London, p15(t), 28, 32(l)
32(r); The National Trust Photographic Library, p35(b) (Andreas von Einsiedel); The Natural History
Museum, London, p38(l); Florence Nightingale Museum, p30(b); The Robert Opie Collection, p13(l),
13(r), 27(t), 30(t); Picturepoint, p43(tl); Royal Academy of Arts, London, p35(t); The Salvation
Army, p29(b); Richard Tames, p18(t), 22(r); Tate Gallery, London, p24, 29(t), 31(t), 37(l);
TRIP, p18(b) (Peter Rauter), 19(b) (Jim Watters);
University of Reading, Rural History Centre,
p12(t); courtesy of the Trustees of the V&A
Museum, p8.

We are unable to trace the copyright holder
of the Great Western Steamship poster on
p40(r) and would appreciate receiving any
information that would enable us to do so.

Endpapers: This printed fabric was designed by William Morris in 1883, it is
called 'Strawberry Thief' (see page 35).

CONTENTS

Who were the Victorians? | 8

Timeline | 10

Where did people get their food? | 12

Did people eat well in Victorian times? | 14

Did they have families like ours? | 16

What sort of houses did people live in? | 18

Did boys and girls go to school? | 20

Who went to work in Victorian times? | 22

What did people do in their spare time? | 24

What did the Victorians wear? | 26

Was religion important? | 28

Did people go to the doctor? | 30

Who ruled the Victorians? | 32

Were there artists in Victorian times? | 34

Did Victorians go to the theatre? | 36

Were there Victorian scientists? | 38

Did people go on long journeys? | 40

What was life like in the army and navy? | 42

Glossary | 44

Index | 45

Words that appear in **bold** can be found in the glossary on page 44.

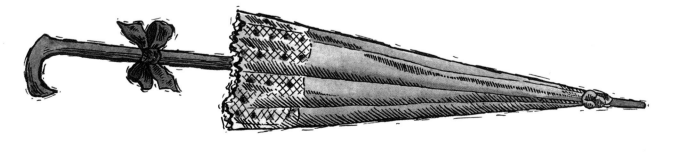

WHO WERE THE VICTORIANS?

Queen Victoria reigned over Britain and its empire from 1837 to 1901. People who lived during this time were called Victorians. The Victorians were very proud of their country's achievements. Educated people felt they were living through a time of exciting progress. But millions of people were poorly fed, and badly housed. Many could not read or write.

▲ BRITAIN ON SHOW

This painting shows the opening ceremony of the Great Exhibition of 1851. Victoria and her husband, Prince Albert, are standing on the platform. New inventions, works of art and products from all over the world were on show.

PENNY POST

Before railways were built, letters went by stagecoach. Railway transport was much cheaper, so postage was cheaper too. It cost one penny to send any letter. This is a 'Penny Black' – the first sticky stamp.

▲ RAILWAY REVOLUTION

During Victoria's reign, many railways were built. Railway travel was four times faster than travel by horse. This painting shows London's Paddington Station. It shows all the different kinds of people who travelled by train. The poor driver had nowhere to shelter from the rain!

▲ SLUMS

The poorest people lived in **slum** housing. They had no proper light, heat or drains. This picture shows slums in London's East End. Often, 40 people might live in one house!

▲ MOTOR CARS

Petrol-engine motor cars were invented in the 1880s. They cost so much money that only the rich could afford them.

TIMELINE

	1830–1840	1841–1850	1851–1860	1861–1870
BRITAIN	1830 Liverpool–Manchester railway opened. 1833 *The Pickwick Papers* by Charles Dickens published. 1837 Victoria becomes Queen. 1840 Penny postage introduced.	1842 New law means women and children cannot work underground. 1845–6 Great Famine in Ireland, millions die. 1847 *Wuthering Heights* by Emily Brontë published. 1848 First Public Health Act passed.	1851 The Great Exhibition takes place. 1852 Houses of Parliament completed. 1859 *The Origin of Species* by Charles Darwin published.	1863 World's first underground railway opens in London. 1866 Undersea cable links Britain and the USA by telegraph. **Houses of Parliament**
THE BRITISH EMPIRE	1833 Slavery banned in the British Empire. Britain takes control of Falkland Islands. 1840 Wars against China and Afghanistan. Britain takes control of New Zealand.	1842 Britain takes control of Hong Kong.	1851 The Australian gold rush begins.	1868 Last convicts sent to Australia.
EUROPE	1831 Polish revolt against Russian rule crushed. 1839 Belgium and Luxembourg become independent.	1848 Year of revolutions in Europe. Karl Marx and Friedrich Engels publish *The Communist Manifesto*.	1852 Napoleon III made Emperor of France. 1854–6 Crimean War.	1864 Red Cross founded in Switzerland. 1867 Swedish chemist, Nobel, invents dynamite. 1870 Italy becomes one country. **Abraham Lincoln**
THE REST OF THE WORLD	1837 Morse code invented (USA). **Morse code**	1846 First operation under **anaesthetic** (USA).	1851 Singer sewing machine invented (USA). 1853 Japan opens to trade.	1861–5 American Civil War. 1865 US President Abraham Lincoln assassinated.

1871–1880	1881–1890	1891–1900	1901–1910
1875 Major Public Health Act is passed.	**1882** Chilled meat imported from Australia for first time.	**1897** Victoria celebrates 60 years as Queen.	**1901** Queen Victoria dies.
1876 Queen Victoria becomes Empress of India.	**1883** *Treasure Island* by Robert Louis Stevenson published.	First Sherlock Holmes story published.	**1902** *Peter Rabbit* by Beatrix Potter published.
1878 Joseph Swan invents light bulb.	**1888** Air-filled tyre invented.	**Sherlock Holmes**	**1908** Old-age **pensions** introduced.
light bulb			
1875 Britain takes control of Suez Canal.	**1882** Britain takes control of Egypt.	**1894** Britain takes control of Uganda.	**1901** Australian **colonies** joined together.
1879 Zulu war in South Africa.	**1886** Gold discovered in South Africa.	**1899–1902** Boer War in South Africa.	**1910** South African colonies joined together.
1871 Germany becomes one country.	**1885** First motor cars made.	**1891–1903** Trans-Siberian Railway built across Russia.	**1901** First Nobel Prizes awarded.
1877–8 War between Russia and Turkey.	**1887–9** Eiffel Tower built in Paris.	**1895** **X-rays** discovered.	**1909** Frenchman Louis Blériot becomes first person to fly across the English Channel.
	Eiffel Tower	**1896** First modern Olympic Games held in Athens.	
1876 Alexander Graham Bell invents telephone in the USA.			**1903** Wright brothers make first manned, powered aircraft flight in the USA.
	1880–90 Europe divides Africa into colonies.	**1894–5** War between China and Japan.	**1904–5** War between Russia and Japan.
	1889 Slavery banned in Brazil.	**1898** War between USA and Spain.	

TOWARDS ONE WORLD

During Queen Victoria's reign, there were many great advances. In the 1830s, it took 11 hours to travel from Bath to London by stagecoach. By the 1860s, it took under two hours to make the same journey by railway. In the 1830s, messages between Britain and the USA were sent on ships across the Atlantic. After 1866, Morse code messages could be sent through a cable on the Atlantic seabed – in seconds. In 1897, Queen Victoria sent a Diamond **Jubilee** message to Australia in under two minutes!

Better transport meant that people and goods could move around the world faster. Millions of people emigrated from Europe. People used railways to move around North and South America, South Africa, Australia and Siberia. Steamships travelled to central Africa and the Amazon.

11

WHERE DID PEOPLE GET THEIR FOOD?

In 1801, 10.5 million people lived in Britain. A hundred years later, the population had risen to 37 million. Farmers had to grow more and more food to feed everyone. Railways and steamships made it easier to bring meat and wheat from abroad. In the country, people visited markets or grew their own vegetables. In towns, they went to shops for food.

▲ THE STEAM PLOUGH

In the above picture, crowds of people watch a steam plough in action. Instead of being pulled by a horse, the plough is being dragged along wires by a steam engine. These machines were made during the 1850s, but they were very expensive. Most farmers could not afford them.

THE COUNTRY MARKET ▶

The painting on the right shows a market in about 1860. Farmers sold fruit, vegetables and even live poultry.

ADVERTISING AND PACKAGING ▼ ▶

Food makers soon realised that brightly coloured labels made their products look better. Sealed packets helped to keep food fresh. The advert on the right boasts that Queen Victoria uses Colman's mustard.

FOODS FROM AROUND THE WORLD ▼

The map below shows some of the countries that sold food to Victorian Britain. British settlers set up many of these food industries. They took sheep to New Zealand and Australia. They also started tea plantations in India and Sri Lanka.

FOOD IN THE USA

The USA invented many snacks that are popular today. These include: doughnuts (1847), chewing gum (1848), canned baked beans (1875) and Coca-Cola (1886). Crisps were invented in the USA in 1853, but didn't reach Britain until 1913!

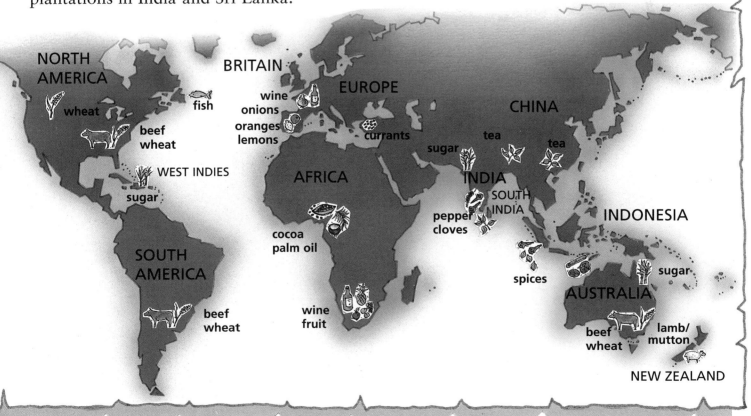

NORTH AMERICA
wheat
fish
beef
wheat
WEST INDIES
sugar

BRITAIN

EUROPE
wine
onions
oranges
lemons
currants

CHINA
tea
sugar
tea

AFRICA
cocoa
palm oil

INDIA
SOUTH INDIA
pepper
cloves

INDONESIA
spices
sugar

SOUTH AMERICA
beef
wheat

wine
fruit

AUSTRALIA
beef
wheat
lamb/mutton

NEW ZEALAND

DID PEOPLE EAT WELL IN VICTORIAN TIMES?

In Victorian times, foreign travel and the wider range of foods

imported from abroad made rich people interested in trying out new foods. For example, British people who had lived in India liked to eat curry and spicy mulligatawny ('pepper water') soup. But the poorest Victorians often had to make do with tea, bread, jam and potatoes. This was a very unhealthy diet.

A COFFEE STALL ▶

The painting on the right shows a coffee stall in London in about 1850. Other street stalls sold hot pies, pastries or roast chestnuts. Stalls like these sold the only hot food that some people ate. Not everyone had a cooker at home – they did not become popular until the 1880s.

◀ HOT MEALS

In factory towns, many women went out to work. It was difficult for them to cook hot meals for their families. Instead, they took a joint of meat or a stew to a bake-house in the morning. On the way home, they collected the cooked meal.

Railways began to bring fish, packed in ice, to factory towns. From the 1860s onwards, people could buy freshly fried fish and chips.

◄ A DINNER PARTY

The painting on the left is from 1884. It shows a very grand dinner party. All of the men wear tail-coats and white ties. The women wear silk dresses. The guest of honour, on the right, is the Prime Minister, William Gladstone.

TABLEWARE ▼

Rich people used different kinds of cutlery and crockery for each dish. The moustache cup below lifted up the moustache when a man drank from it.

THE CO-OP

The Co-operative movement was started in Rochdale, Lancashire in 1844. It tried to help poorer people by selling basic goods cheaply. The Co-op did not make a profit.

Moustache cup

Egg cups and spoons on a stand

Sandwich servers

SOUP KITCHENS ►

The picture on the right shows a soup kitchen. These were set up to give free food to the poorest people. They fed unemployed adults and homeless children. Women with servants often filled their spare time working for charities.

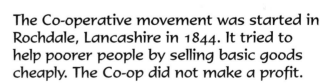

DID THEY HAVE FAMILIES LIKE OURS?

Most Victorian families were large. In the 1860s, the average farm labourer had seven children. Single men often lived with families who were glad to have lodgers for the extra income they brought. Wealthy families were also big, with many servants to look after them. Unmarried aunts or sisters often lived with these families too.

Doll

▲ A FAMILY OCCASION

Victorian people thought that family life was a great blessing. This painting from 1856 shows a birthday party in a wealthy family. The children have been given a glass of sherry as a special treat.

◄ HOME, SWEET HOME

Girls were often given doll's houses because they were expected to stay at home as a wife and mother. They were not expected to go out to work. Boys might have been given a fort or a model farmyard to play with.

Doll's house

▲ QUEUING FOR SHELTER

These homeless people are queuing for free shelter for the night. When the painting was first shown in 1874, it shocked the wealthy people who saw it. They had no idea how difficult life was for poor people.

 ## A SERVANT'S WORK

In 1851, there were a million servants in Britain. Ninety per cent of these servants were female. One of the worst jobs was being a scullery maid. She had to light the coal fires and wash the dishes. Most ladies' dresses couldn't be washed. They had to be unmade and remade every time they were cleaned.

Many cleaning products were home-made. To clean silk or ribbons, servants mixed together 300ml gin, 225g honey, 225g soft soap and 300ml water.

▲ ORPHAN CHILDREN

Most orphans had lost their mother and father because of accidents or diseases. Some were deserted by desperate parents. The picture above shows an orphanage at a meal-time. These children were lucky. Other orphans were sent to work in factories, where they were treated badly.

WHAT SORT OF HOUSES DID PEOPLE LIVE IN?

Before the railways, it was very expensive to transport building materials over long distances. This meant that most houses were built with local materials. Railways made transport much cheaper. Red bricks and Welsh roof-slates were now used all over the country. By 1900, new homes had gas lighting and drainage. Some of them even had an inside toilet!

◀ A GENTLEMAN'S HOME

The picture on the left shows a country house of the 1830s. Fast railway travel meant that wealthy people could spend the weekend in the countryside. Here, they held house parties. Guests came from the towns to enjoy shooting, hunting, dining and dancing.

A COAL MINER'S COTTAGE ▶

The living room of this Durham miner's home has a large **range**. The fire heated the room, while meals were cooked in the oven. As machines replaced craftsmen in factories, goods became cheaper to produce. More and more people could afford to fill their homes with ornaments like the china dogs in this room.

◄ UNDER THE RAILWAY ARCHES

This picture shows houses for poor people in London in the 1870s. The houses look grim and dreary. But there are proper windows and drainpipes. There was a **scullery** behind each house. This was a tiny room with a chimney where families could heat water for washing and baths. Almost everyone rented their homes in Victorian times.

NEW HOME COMFORTS

Gas lighting gave a better and cheaper light than candles. Electric lighting was invented in the 1880s, but it was still rare outside big cities until after 1900. Cheaper cast iron meant that more families could afford a mangle. This squeezed water out of wet clothes. But only people who were well off could afford gadgets like coffee grinders. Carpet sweepers were slow to become popular in Britain. Rich people who could afford them had servants to do the work instead.

Gas light

Coffee grinder

Carpet sweeper

▲ MANSION FLATS

In Scotland, people had been used to living in multi-storey **tenements** since the 1600s. However, well-off people in England didn't like the idea of living without gardens. It wasn't until the 1880s that the first 'mansion flats' were built in London. The flats were ideal for wealthy people with small families or no children.

DID BOYS AND GIRLS GO TO SCHOOL?

Educated people were not sure that everyone should learn to read and write. They thought that poor people should be able to read the Bible. But they didn't want them to read other things – like newspapers that wanted reforms. Church-based charities ran schools. Then in 1870, the government became responsible for education.

◄ PUBLIC SCHOOLS

The rich paid to send their sons to 'public schools'. The picture on the left shows Rugby School. This school set new standards by teaching French, maths and history as well as Latin and Greek. Daughters were often taught at home by a **governess**.

DAME SCHOOLS ►

The painting on the right shows a 'dame school'. This type of school was found in most villages. For many poor children, it was the only type of school they would have the chance to go to. The 'dame' was usually a poor widow who earned a few pennies by teaching children. The children were all taught together, with very few books and little equipment.

BOARD SCHOOLS ▶

'Board schools' were paid for by local taxes. In the painting on the right, all the pupils are in one room. But there are two trained teachers, proper blackboards and desks.

BEHAVE YOURSELF! ▼

In Victorian schools, cheekiness and disobedience were punished with beating. **Dunce's** caps or sleeve badges like these were used to shame lazy, dirty and naughty children.

Sleeve badges

▲ TEACHING BY PUPILS

In Victorian times, there was a shortage of trained teachers. Schools run on the 'monitorial system', like the one above, helped to solve this problem. The teacher would teach each lesson to a team of older pupils – the monitors. The monitors would then repeat the lesson to younger pupils.

EDUCATION FOR ALL

Between 1833 and 1900, the government increased spending on education by a huge amount. By 1900, almost 90 per cent of children aged five to 11 were enrolled in a school. But the number of children who actually went to school was lower. In the countryside, children did not attend school when there was work to do in the fields. Only four out of ten children were at school between the ages of 12 and 14.

WHO WENT TO WORK IN VICTORIAN TIMES?

In Victorian times, many people began to work in mines and factories. But traditional skills and crafts were still important. For example, in 1851, there were more cobblers than coal miners. Some work was risky. People who made cotton and woollen cloth in factories worked with dangerous machines. In mines and on farms, whole families were often hired to work. The father acted as the children's boss.

◄ THE TRADE UNIONS

A trade union is a group of employees who work together to protect their rights. Many were formed in the 1830s and 1840s, but most collapsed because they were badly led. One successful trade union was the Amalgamated Society of Engineers – their membership certificate is shown on the left. Skilled workers formed the best unions. Often, they could read and write and ran their organisation well. Only workers who had trained for seven years could join unions like this. They wanted to limit the number of skilled workers, to protect their own jobs and keep wages high.

DOWN ON THE FARM ►

The photograph of haymaking on the right was taken around 1900. At this time, much farm work was still done by hand and using horse power. Steam-powered machinery was too expensive.

FACTORY LIFE ▶

The painting on the right shows women factory workers in 1874. They are resting during their midday meal break. Because there were no factory canteens, the women have brought their own food and drink. In the background, tall chimneys pour smoke into the air. On the right, there is a gas lamp, to light the way home at night.

A BLACKSMITH'S TOOLS

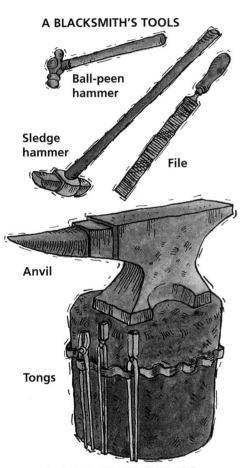

Ball-peen hammer

Sledge hammer

File

Anvil

Tongs

▲ A BLACKSMITH'S WORK

Blacksmiths repaired farm tools and carts, shoed horses and made wrought-iron gates.

MEN'S WORK, WOMEN'S WORK

In Victorian times, many jobs were thought to be 'male' or 'female'. In 1851, seven out of every eight farm workers were men. Eight out of every nine domestic servants were women. Equal numbers of men and women worked in the cotton industry. But nearly all builders were men and nearly all dressmakers were women.

▲ CHILDREN'S WORK

At the beginning of Victoria's reign, children of five and six were sent down mines and others were sent up chimneys. The boy in the photograph above is learning to make shoes. By 1900, laws banned the worst treatment of children.

WHAT DID PEOPLE DO IN THEIR SPARE TIME?

By Victoria's reign, activities became more organised and less cruel. Tormenting bulls and bears with dogs for sport was banned. Inter-school sports became more popular. This led to agreed rules for different games. Boxers stopped fighting with their bare knuckles – they now began to wear gloves. In towns, parks were built for families to enjoy the fresh air.

ON THE MOVE ▶

The penny-farthing bicycle gave the rider a terrific view, with riders 1.5 metres off the ground! Cycling became really popular in the 1880s, when the modern safety bicycle was invented.

▼ DERBY DAY

The colourful painting below shows huge crowds of both rich and poor Victorians. They have come to watch the famous horse race at Epsom Downs.

Penny farthing

THE SEASIDE ▶

The painting on the right shows Brighton in the 1880s. The **promenade** was built so that visitors could breathe the sea air without stumbling on the beach. Invalids were often told to take a seaside holiday for their health. Railways made it easier for Victorians to get to the coast. Even working people could afford a day trip to the seaside.

Ball

Bucket

Spade

A NEW GAME ▼

Lawn tennis was invented in the 1870s. It was an ideal game for well off Victorians to play in their own garden. The game was played very gently. This meant that women could join in, despite their tight, heavy clothes.

MILESTONES IN LEISURE

The first town park is laid out in Preston, Lancashire. 1834

Sussex forms the first County Cricket Club. 1839

The first Rugby Football Club is formed in London. 1843

The first children's playground is laid out in Manchester. 1859

The first athletics club is formed in London. 1863

The first international soccer match takes place. Result: England 0 – Scotland 0. 1872

Snooker is invented at a British Army officers' club in India. 1875

The first Test match is played between England and Australia. 1877

The first modern Olympic games are held in Athens, Greece. 1896

WHAT DID THE VICTORIANS WEAR?

Victorians wanted clothes that would last. The poor had to make their clothes last – they could not afford new ones. The rich wanted well-made clothes to show that they could afford good quality. Underclothes were now made of cotton instead of linen. This was easier to wash. Men and women of all classes wore boots instead of shoes. The poor wore woollen shawls to keep them warm.

◀ A MAN OF FASHION

This gentleman was photographed in about 1860. He would never go out without his hat, cane and gloves. His jacket, waistcoat and trousers are like a modern suit, but do not match. He wears a **cravat** instead of a modern tie.

▼ CHILDREN'S CLOTHES

The photograph below shows working-class children from around 1890. The girls wear smocks to protect their dresses. The boys' clothes are made of tough corduroy or tweed. Everyone wears a hat.

In Victorian times, it was not respectable to go out without a hat. Lace, ribbons and real bird feathers were used to decorate women's hats.

Upper-class men wore shiny silk top hats. Middle-class men wore bowler hats. Working men and boys wore soft, flat cloth caps.

▲ CORSETS

Tight corsets made of whalebone or steel made breathing difficult – the wearer often felt faint and dizzy. But women ignored doctors' advice not to wear corsets because it was fashionable for them to have tiny waists.

WOMEN'S FASHIONS ▶

Wealthy Victorian women had separate outfits for morning, afternoon and evening, and for indoors and outside. This meant that they spent hours each day dressing and changing. Most rich women had a personal maid, who helped them to dress and looked after their hair.

WAS RELIGION IMPORTANT?

Thousands of churches and chapels were built in Victorian times. Parliament spent a third of its time talking about religious questions. Religion affected which type of school children attended. There were also strict laws to control what people could and couldn't do on Sundays. But only one in three Victorians went to church.

▲ A CHRISTIAN RULER

In the above painting, Queen Victoria presents a Bible to an African king. This event probably never took place, but it shows that the Victorians thought it was their duty to spread Christianity around the world. Missionaries set up Christian communities, schools and hospitals in Africa, eastern Asia and the Pacific. This increased Europeans' knowledge of other languages and customs.

◄ A SHOCKING PICTURE

This painting shows Christ in his parents' house. It caused a storm of protest when it was first shown in 1850. Charles Dickens thought it was too realistic and that the people were ugly.

Stained-glass window

STAINED GLASS ►

Many new Victorian churches were decorated with stained glass windows. They showed scenes from the Bible or told stories about holy people. The richly coloured windows were often put on the western or eastern side of the church. When the light shone through these windows, they looked stunning.

ROMAN CATHOLICS

Britain became a Protestant country in the sixteenth century. Until 1829, Catholics were forbidden to become MPs or judges. After this time, the number of Catholics grew, especially when Irish immigrants arrived in Britain. By 1840, there were 700,000 Catholics in Britain.

◄ THE SALVATION ARMY

William Booth founded the Salvation Army in 1865. In the picture on the left, he is speaking to a packed meeting. He wanted to help people who wouldn't usually go to church. William Booth was against drinking. He thought people should emigrate to find better lives for themselves.

DID PEOPLE GO TO THE DOCTOR?

During Victoria's reign, medical care improved enormously. There were more trained doctors and nurses, and more hospitals and clinics. Laws stopped people from pretending to be doctors without proper qualifications. From 1846, anaesthetics made surgery far less painful. Antiseptics cut down the risk of infection. X-rays were discovered in 1895. They allowed doctors to see inside the body without surgery.

◄ PILLS, POTIONS AND GADGETS

New medicines and methods of curing illnesses appeared every year. Even doctors found it difficult to tell the difference between a good new idea and a bad one. The advertisement on the left claims that a special electric belt will cure all sorts of medical problems including indigestion and sleeplessness.

▼ FLORENCE NIGHTINGALE

Florence Nightingale was a nurse. She became famous for her work with the wounded during the Crimean War (1854–6). Here, Florence sits among a group of nurses at the training school she started at St Thomas's Hospital, London.

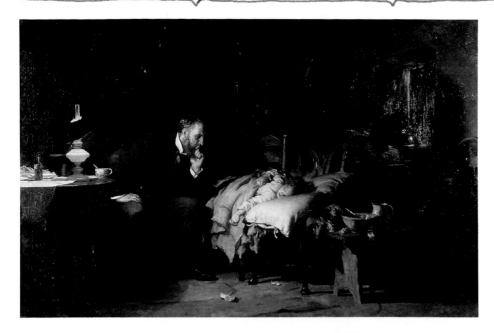

◀ A SICK CHILD

Most Victorian families lost at least one child from illness or accident. The rich could afford to send their sick children to hospital, but often nursed them at home. In hospital, there was a risk of catching illnesses from other patients.

▲ A CHILDREN'S WARD

The photograph above shows a light, airy children's ward at Guy's Hospital in London, around 1900. This was a surgical ward, where children came for operations. There were toys to encourage the children to play and get fit again after their treatment. As late as 1900, 150 babies out of every 1,000 born died before their first birthday. Many died from common childhood diseases like measles or whooping cough.

DENTISTRY

Anaesthetics made dentistry less painful, but it could still be very unpleasant. The newly invented dentist's drill was operated by pedal power. It went very slowly...

Dentist's pliers

Scalpel

WHO RULED THE COUNTRY?

At the beginning of Victoria's reign, rich landowners were the most powerful group in Parliament. Then, Sir Robert Peel became Prime Minister. His family had made money in business. By the 1890s, a few working men were being elected. Trade unions supported them.

▲ REIGNING, NOT RULING

Queen Victoria had to pass the laws that the Prime Minister and Parliament wanted. She did not believe that women should be given the vote!

▲ A WISE ADVISER

Victoria's husband was Albert, a German prince. He was known as the Prince Consort. They had a very happy marriage and Victoria almost always followed his advice.

HOW THEY VOTED ▶

The poster on the right shows how people in Suffolk towns voted in 1835. Voting was made in public. This made it easy for landlords and employers to bully people into voting the way they wanted. Voting became secret in 1872.

◀ TWO GREAT RIVALS

This picture shows Gladstone (right, standing) and Disraeli (left). The two men were both Prime Ministers at different times and were great rivals. Gladstone tried to cut taxes and improve conditions in Ireland. Disraeli gained control of the Suez Canal. He made Queen Victoria, Empress of India.

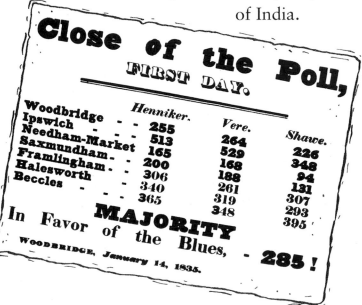

	Henniker.	Vere.	Shawe.
Woodbridge	255	264	226
Ipswich	513	529	348
Needham-Market	165	168	94
Saxmundham	200	188	131
Framlingham	306	261	307
Halesworth	340	319	293
Beccles	365	348	395

Close of the Poll, FIRST DAY.

In Favor of the Blues, MAJORITY - 285 !

WOODBRIDGE, January 14, 1835.

REFORMING PARLIAMENT

At the beginning of the nineteenth century, only some men were allowed to vote. Then, a law in 1832 allowed big, new cities like Birmingham and Manchester to elect MPs for the first time. In 1867 and 1884 more laws were passed to allow more men the vote. In 1883, laws were passed against bribing voters.

▲ VOTES FOR WOMEN!

The women in this photograph want the right to vote – the suffrage. They were called suffragettes and broke the law to gain publicity. Women aged 30 finally got the vote in 1918.

WERE THERE ARTISTS IN VICTORIAN TIMES?

From the 1840s, Victorian artists had new competition – photography. It was now possible to make accurate pictures without drawing or painting.

So, many artists chose to paint pictures with strong colour or lighting effects. They also painted scenes with quick movement or pictures of historical or imaginary events. The camera could do none of these things.

ART ON SHOW ▼

The painting below shows visitors at an art exhibition making up their minds about a new picture. Some people sold paintings for large amounts. Others put their pictures on show and charged people to look at them. By 1900, most big cities had opened art galleries where local people could see paintings free of charge.

◀ AN ARTIST IN HIS STUDIO

This painting, called 'The Sleepy Model', is a self-portrait by the painter W.P. Frith. The model was an Irish girl who sold oranges in the street. Frith was well trained, hard working and very successful.

Fabric design by William Morris

PHOTOGRAPHY

Photography was invented in France in 1826. In 1840, the Englishman W.H. Fox Talbot discovered how to print photographs on paper.

Camera

The first flash photograph was taken in 1850. In 1888, American George Eastman invented the first cheap, simple camera.

▲ ART AND DESIGN

William Morris was a Victorian painter who became an interior designer. He designed the above bedroom. Many of his patterns are based on flowers, plants and birds. William Morris wallpapers can still be bought today. The first and last pages in this book show a William Morris design.

DID VICTORIANS GO TO THE THEATRE?

During the early years of Victoria's reign, theatre-going was not very respectable. Audiences were sometimes rowdy. Actors and actresses would

not have been welcome guests in many homes. Opera, ballet and concerts were much more acceptable to wealthy people. The comic operas written by Gilbert and Sullivan were very popular.

▲ STREET ENTERTAINERS

Poor people enjoyed watching street entertainers. They often played musical instruments, juggled or did acrobatics. The man in ropes shown above is an escape artist. Most street entertainers were always on the move. They travelled from one country fair to the next.

CHARLES DICKENS'S
DRAMATIC READINGS
AS READ IN AMERICA.

▲ A KEEN THEATRE-GOER

The novelist Charles Dickens (1812–70) loved the theatre. When he was young, he went to the theatre two or three times a week. Before he became a writer, he wanted to be an actor. When he was older, he gave brilliant readings from his novels in Britain and the USA.

◀ THE GREATEST ACTRESS OF HER DAY

Ellen Terry (1847–1928) first acted on stage at the age of nine. The portrait on the left shows Ellen playing the part of Lady Macbeth in Shakespeare's *Macbeth*.

MUSIC HALLS ▼

In music halls there was often as much action in the audience as there was on stage. There were short scenes from plays rather than whole plays. There might also be a series of acts by singers, acrobats or conjurors.

A KNIGHT OF THE THEATRE

Sir Henry Irving (1838–1905) was the first actor ever to be knighted for his work in the theatre. He made Shakespeare's plays popular with audiences again and often acted with Ellen Terry.

Sir Henry Irving and Ellen Terry

HOME ENTERTAINMENT

Brightly coloured toy theatres were popular in Victorian times.

WERE THERE VICTORIAN SCIENTISTS?

Great discoveries in science and technology were made during the nineteenth century. Electricity was used to send messages by telegraph. It also provided power for industry and light for streets and homes. Industry began to use new materials like rubber and aluminium. In 1835, Charles Babbage invented a mechanical calculator – the ancestor of the modern computer. Schools and colleges also began to teach science.

▲ ANGELS OR APES?

Charles Darwin (1809–82) wrote books explaining how living things had **evolved** from simpler living things over millions of years. Many Victorians thought this idea disagreed with the Bible. They made fun of Darwin in the above cartoon.

▲ WHO IS THAT SPEAKING?

The telephone was invented by Alexander Graham Bell, in 1876. In the photograph, the Scotsman shows how his invention works. Businesses were quick to see the value of Bell's telephone.

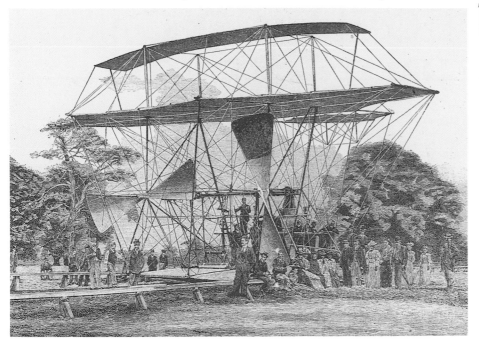

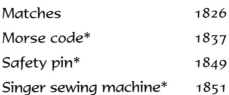
Typewriter

▲ A FLYING MACHINE

Throughout history, many people have tried to fly. Victorians tried too. But experimental flying machines like the one shown above were either too heavy or too fragile. It was not until 1903 that the first successful manned, powered flight took place in the USA. Wilbur Wright watched his brother Orville fly 36 metres – less than the length of a modern passenger jet!

Sewing-machine

Gas fires	1856
Typewriter*	1867
Toilet roll*	1871
Wristwatch°	1880
Electric iron*	1882
Dishwasher*	1886
Electric torch	1891
Zip*	1893
Safety razor*	1895
Electric washing machine*	1901

▲ A TRIUMPH OF ENGINEERING

Isambard Kingdom Brunel (1806–59) was one of the greatest engineers of all time. This painting shows the railway bridge he designed to cross the River Tamar in Devon.

* US invention

° French invention

DID PEOPLE GO ON LONG JOURNEYS?

The invention of railways and steamships made transport faster, safer and more reliable. On good roads, stagecoaches could only travel at 12 kilometres an hour. In 1830, the first railway carried passengers from Liverpool to Manchester at over 30 kilometres an hour. By the 1850s, railway trains travelled at over 80 kilometres an hour! The fastest sailing ships took 12 days to cross the Atlantic Ocean. Steamships did the journey in less than eight days.

▲ EMIGRATION

This painting shows **emigrants** leaving Britain to travel to Australia. Most emigrants were young people. They thought they had a chance of a better life in countries where there were more jobs and free land. Between 1815 and 1914, about 15 million people left Britain and Ireland.

SAIL AND STEAM ▲

The poster above advertises a steamship service between Bristol and New York. If it was windy, steamships often used their sails to save fuel.

BUSINESS AND PLEASURE

Railways made transport cheaper. This meant that businesses could buy materials and sell their goods over much greater distances. Mail-order shopping became possible. Instead of being tiring and often dangerous, travel could be a pleasure. By the 1880s, trains even had lighting, heating and corridors!

HORSE OR TRAIN TRAVEL? ▶

The poster on the right is from 1845. It advertises a horse-drawn bus service to the coast. But horses could not compete with the speed of railways. Soon, they made deliveries and carried passengers within towns instead.

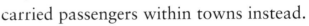

MILESTONES IN TRAVEL

First passenger railway	1825	First electric locomotive	1879
First London omnibus	1829	First electric tram	1888
First underground railway	1863	First London–Brighton car rally	1896

◀ THE FIRST TRAVEL AGENT

Thomas Cook (1808–92) was a printer and preacher who invented modern tourism. In 1841, he hired a train to take 570 passengers to hear a lecture against drinking. By 1856, he was organising tours around Europe. None of this would have been possible without cheap, reliable railway travel. Soon, the company booked hotels as well as arranging travel.

WHAT WAS LIFE LIKE IN THE ARMY AND NAVY?

During Victoria's reign, Britain only fought one large war. This was the Crimean War (1854–6) in Russia. But the British army fought a small war somewhere in the British Empire almost every year. Soldiers were badly paid. Until 1881, they could even be punished by flogging. The Royal Navy was much more popular than the army.

▲ A TERRIBLE DEFEAT

The army did not win every battle. The painting above shows a battle at Isandhlwana in South Africa. British soldiers were attacked by Zulu warriors. Many British soldiers died.

 **FURTHER AND FASTER**

During the 1840s, better guns were invented. The new rifles could fire bullets a distance of 1 kilometre instead of 200 metres. Machine guns were invented around 1850. They could fire more bullets per minute than 40 rifles. Machine guns meant that the British could conquer larger areas with fewer troops.

NEW UNIFORMS ▼

Bright uniforms were replaced in 1857. The new khaki uniforms made it easier for troops to stay hidden.

▲ THE CHARGE OF THE LIGHT BRIGADE

During the Crimean War, a group of 600 soldiers were ordered to attack a group of Russians. Almost half the men were killed. The event was retold in Lord Tennyson's famous poem – *The Charge of the Light Brigade*.

SHIPS, SHIPS, SHIPS! ▶

In 1897, the navy celebrated Queen Victoria's 60th year on the throne. If the 150 ships in the **Jubilee** procession had been put end to end, they would have measured 11 kilometres!

Early machine gun

◀ THE VICTORIA CROSS

The highest British award for bravery is the Victoria Cross. It is awarded very rarely. Since 1856, around 1,350 people have been given the 'VC'.

Victoria Cross

GLOSSARY

ANAESTHETIC A drug or gas used by doctors to stop a patient feeling pain.

ANTISEPTIC A substance that stops infections.

COBBLER A person who mends shoes.

COLONY (COLONIES) A group of people who settle in a new country but are still ruled by their homeland.

CRAVAT A kind of scarf worn around the neck by men.

DUNCE A pupil who is slow at learning.

EMIGRANT Someone who goes to another country to live forever.

EMPIRE A large group of countries ruled over by a single country.

EVOLVE When an animal or plant develops over time into another form of animal or plant.

FLOGGING Beating with a whip or cane.

GOVERNESS A woman teacher who teaches children at home.

IMMIGRANT Someone who has arrived from another country to live.

JUBILEE A special anniversary, such as when a king or queen has reigned for 50 or 60 years.

LOCOMOTIVE The engine part of a train. It pulls the carriages along.

MANSION FLAT A large, luxurious flat.

OMNIBUS A horse-drawn carriage that carried passengers along a set route.

PENSION Money people live on after they have retired.

PROMENADE A paved walkway along a seafront.

RANGE A large cooking stove.

SCULLERY A small room at the back of the house for washing dishes and dirty clothes.

SETTLER Someone who goes to a different place and makes it their home.

SLUM An area of very poor housing.

SUFFRAGETTES Women who fought to get the vote.

TECHNOLOGY Studying machines and how they work.

TENEMENT Block of flats often found in Scottish cities.

X-RAY A special type of photograph of the inside of someone's body.

INDEX

advertisement 13, 30, 40, 41
aircraft 11, 39
Albert, Prince Consort 8, 32
army 42–3
art 8, 34–5

bake-houses 14
Bell, Alexander Graham 11, 38
Bible 20, 28, 29, 38
bicycles 24
blacksmiths 23
Booth, William 29
Brunel, Isambard Kingdom 39
buses 41

cameras 34, 35
cars 9, 11, 41
children 10, 15, 16–17, 20–1, 22, 23, 26, 28, 31
churches 28–9
clothes 17, 26–7, 43
Co-operative movement 15
coal mining 18, 22, 23
coffee stalls 14
Cook, Thomas 41
cooking 14, 18
Crimean War 10, 30, 42, 43

Darwin, Charles 10, 38
dentists 31
Dickens, Charles 10, 29, 36
Disraeli, Benjamin 33
doctors 30–1

education 20–1, 38
elections 32, 33
electricity 19, 36, 38, 39
emigration 11, 22, 29, 40
engineering 39
evolution 38

factories 17, 18, 22–3
families 16–17, 19, 22, 24, 31
farming 12, 22, 23
food 12–15, 23
Frith, W.P. 35

Gladstone, William 15, 33
Great Exhibition 8, 10
guns 41–3

holidays 25, 41
hospitals 30, 31
houses 9, 16, 18–19

imported food 12, 13, 14
inventions 8, 19, 38–9
Irving, Sir Henry 37

leisure 24–5
lighting 11, 19, 23, 38, 41

mansion flats 19
medicine 30–1
missionaries 28
Morris, William 35
Morse code 10, 11, 39
music halls 37

navy 42–3
Nightingale, Florence 30
nurses 30

operas 36
orphans 17

Parliament 10, 28, 32
Peel, Sir Robert 32
photography 34, 35
ploughing 12
politicians 32–3

poor people 9, 14, 15, 17, 20, 24, 26, 36
postal system 8, 10, 11

railways 9, 10, 11, 12, 18, 25, 39, 40, 41
religion 28–9

Salvation Army 29
schools 20–1, 28, 38
science 38–9
seaside 25
servants 15, 16, 17, 19, 23, 27
ships 11, 12, 40, 43
slums 9
soup kitchens 15
sport 24–5
stagecoaches 11, 40
street entertainers 36
suffragettes 33

teachers 20, 21
telegraph 10, 11
telephones 11, 38
Terry, Ellen 37
theatres 36–7
toys 16, 31, 37
trade unions 22, 32
travel 9, 11, 14, 40–1

United States of America 10, 11, 13, 39

Victoria, Queen 8, 9, 10, 11, 13, 23, 24, 28, 30, 32, 33, 36, 43
Victoria Cross 43

work 14, 17, 21, 22–3
Wright brothers 11, 39